FRANZ LISZT
Un sospiro (A Sigh), S. 144:3
from *Trois études de concert*

Maurice Hinson, Editor

About the Music

Form: Theme and Variations. The opening theme (measures 3–5) is repeated several times with ornamental variations and two interspersed cadenzas.

A = measures 1–12; A^1 = 13–22; A^2 = 22–30; A^3 = 30–37; cadenza = 37–38;

A^4 = 38–51; cadenza = 52; A^5 = 53–62; coda = 62–77.

Un sospiro, S. 144:3, is the third of *Trois études de concert*, published in 1849. These works were composed soon after Liszt retired as a traveling virtuoso and settled in Weimar. In an early French edition they were titled *Trois caprices poétiques* and *Un sospiro* does seem more like a poem than an exercise.

The lovely pentatonic melody is embedded in rolling arpeggio-like figuration so that almost each melodic note is played by alternating hands. The listener should hear only a smoothly flowing line. The hand-crossings and flowing melody are the technical challenges to be solved.

Liszt made two revisions:

1. A slow chordal section was inserted at the end of the second cadenza, prior to the final statement of the main theme before measure 53 of this edition.

before measure 53 of this edition

2. An alternative ending based on a whole-tone scale in the bass was added (replacing measures 72–77 of this edition).

replaces measures 72–77 of this edition

About This Edition

This edition is based on *Franz Liszt's Musikalische Werke herausgegeben von der Franz Liszt-Stiftung*, Series II, edited by Ferruccio Busoni (Leipzig: Breitkopf & Härtel, 1910–11). The traditional style pedal symbol is used to display Liszt's pedal indications (𝓟𝑒𝑑.) and releases (✳) in measures 1–5, while modern pedal notation (└──∧──┘) is used to display editorial pedal indications. Wavy lines (〰〰) indicate flutter pedal. *Armonioso* (above measure 1) suggests using considerable pedal throughout the piece. Fingerings are editorial. A few less familiar Italian terms have been translated into English. The "S." number refers to the catalogue of Liszt's works by Humphrey Searle, prepared for *Grove* V, 1954, revised and updated by him for *The New Grove Dictionary*, vol. 11, 1980.

Second Edition
Copyright © MMIII by Alfred Music

This edition is dedicated to
Dr. Betty Sue Shepherd, with
admiration and appreciation.

Maurice Hinson

Un sospiro
(A Sigh)
from *Trois études de concert*

Allegro affettuoso (Lively with tender expression)

armonioso
(harmonious)

Franz Liszt (1811–1886)
S. 144:3

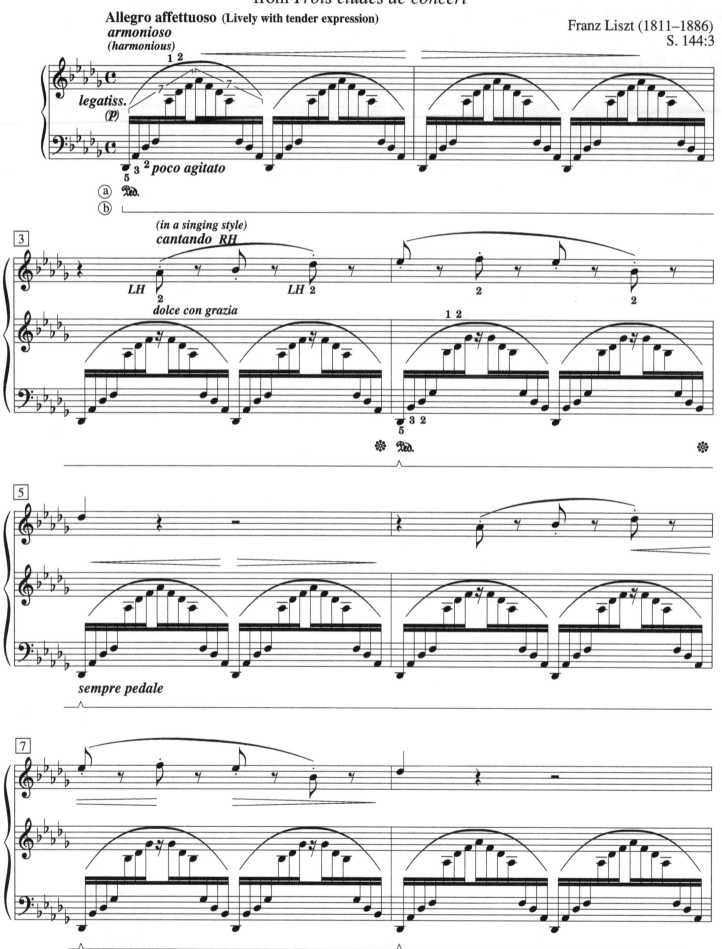

ⓐ Liszt's pedal indications.

ⓑ Editor's pedal indications.

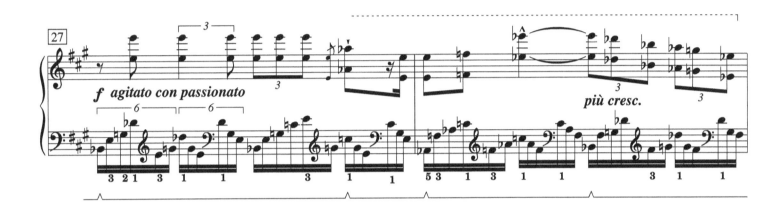

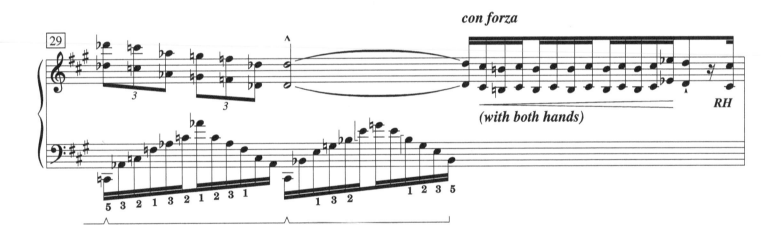

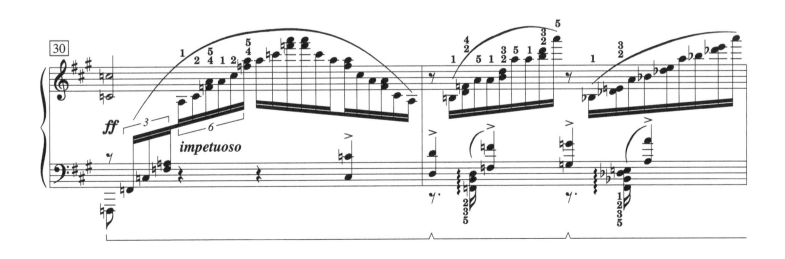

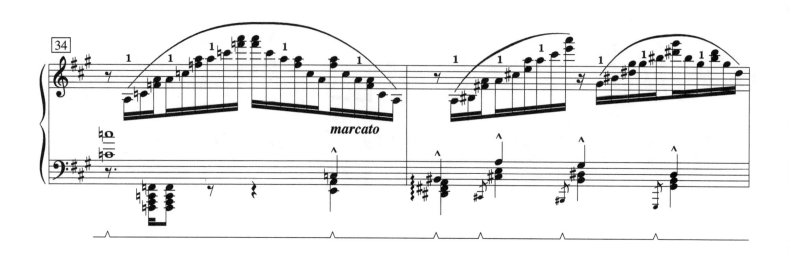

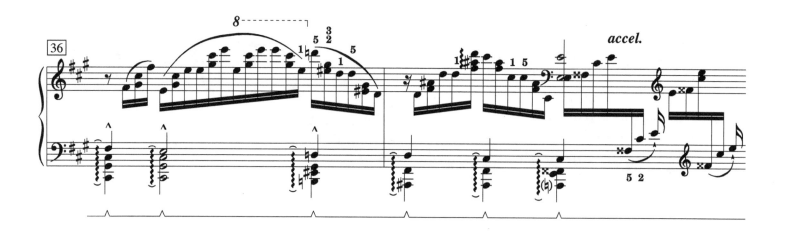

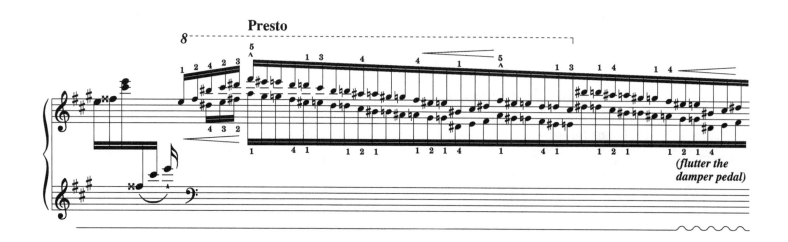

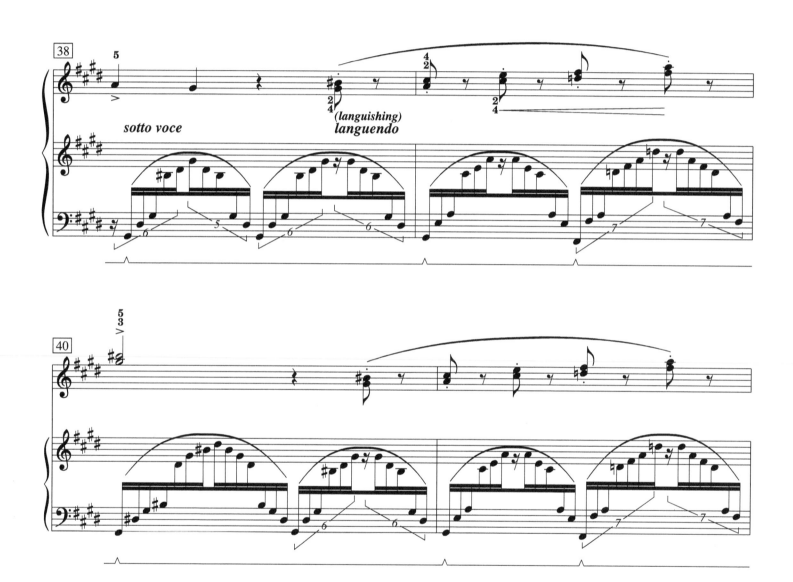

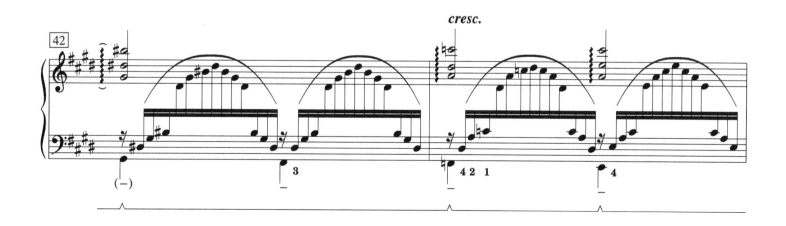

(light and rapid)
leggierissimo volante

accel.

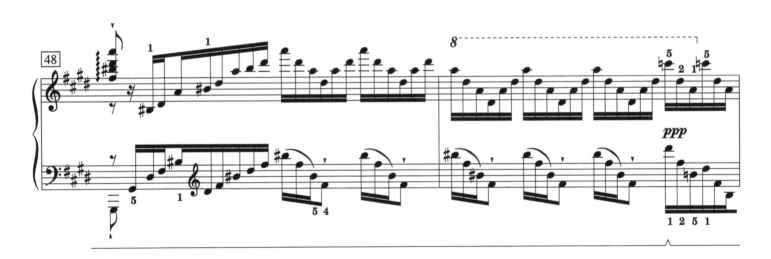

ppp

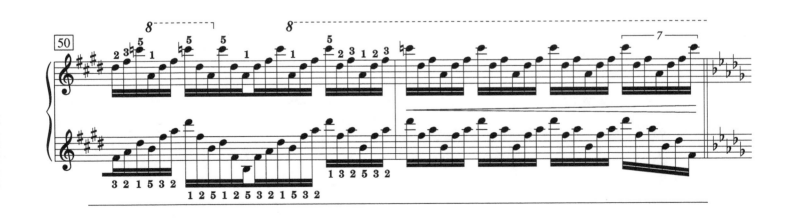

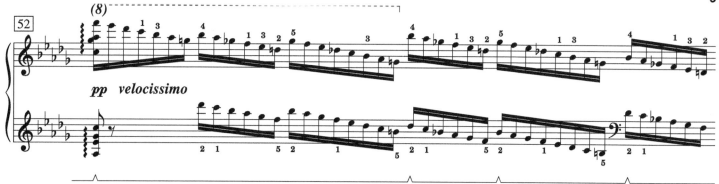

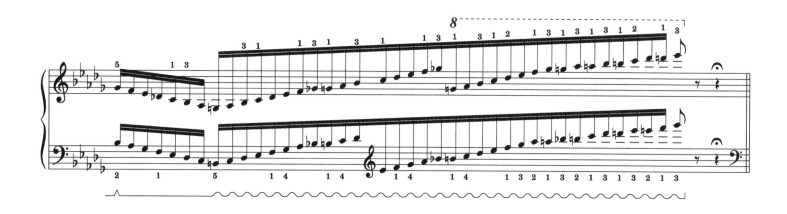

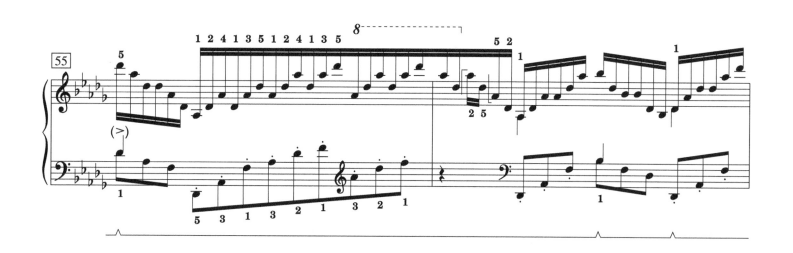

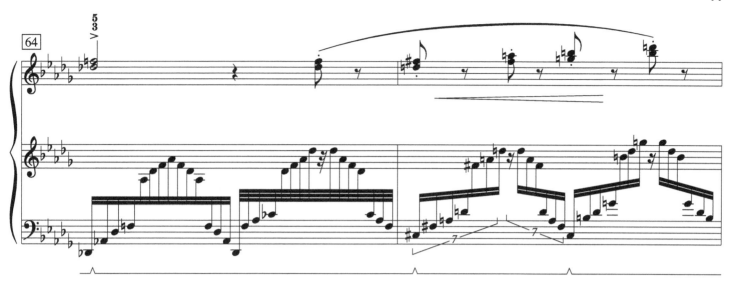

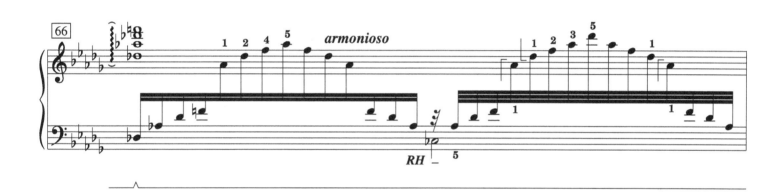

armonioso

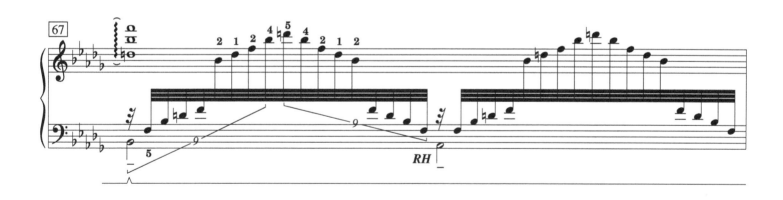

poco a poco rallentando

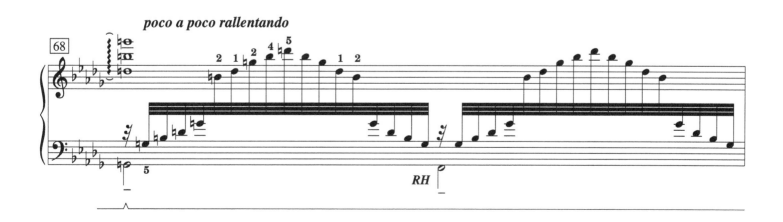

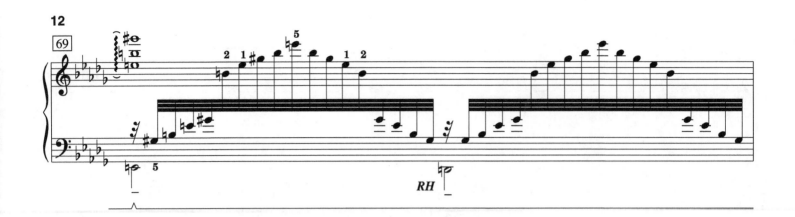

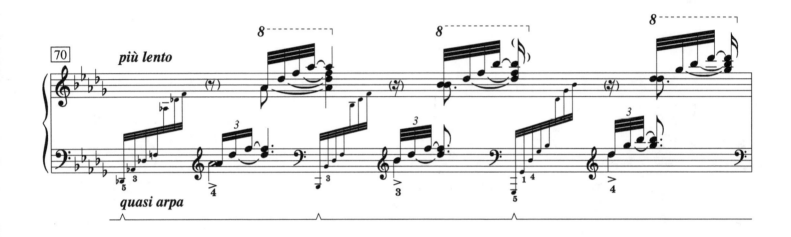

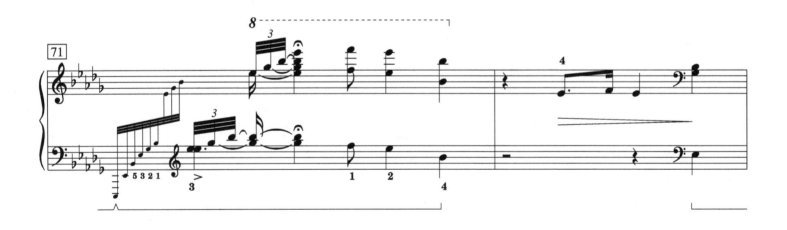

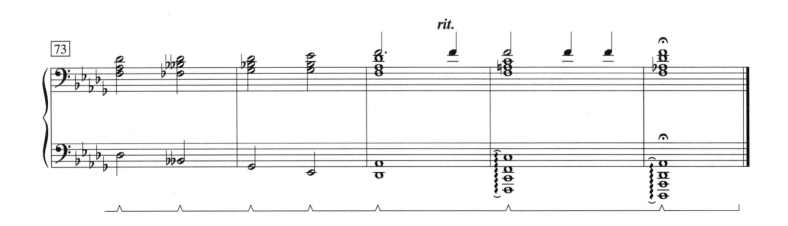